M000312048

Dominie
Chapter
Books

Sam King
and Little Bull

By Trevor Wilson
Illustrated by Peter Wilks

🜛 Dominie Press, Inc.

Publisher: Raymond Yuen
Editor: Bob Rowland
Designer: Mark Deutman
Illustrator: Peter Wilks
Cover Designer: Carol Anne Craft

Copyright ©1999 Dominie Press, Inc. All rights reserved. No part of this publication may be reproduced or transmitted in any form or by any means without permission in writing from the publisher. Reproduction of any part of this book, through photocopy, recording, or any electronic or mechanical retrieval system, without the written permission of the publisher, is an infringement of the copyright law.

Published by:

ᴘ Dominie Press, Inc.

1949 Kellogg Avenue
Carlsbad, California 92008 USA

ISBN 0-7685-0322-1

Printed in Singapore by PH Productions Pte Ltd

1 2 3 4 5 6 PH 01 00 99

TABLE OF CONTENTS

Chapter One
Sam King Rides a King-Size Machine   4

Chapter Two
A Bulldozer of His Own   12

Chapter Three
Just a Piece of Junk?   20

Chapter Four
Little Bull Comes to Life!   24

Chapter Five
Sam King and Little Bull: One Great Team!   32

Chapter One

Sam King Rides a King-Size Machine

Sam King worked on a bulldozer. A huge bulldozer. A stupendous bulldozer. An enormous bulldozer. A great, powerful machine that throbbed and roared as if to tell the world how strong it was.

It *was* strong, too. It could push over trees and level a house flat in a minute or two. But Sam didn't do either of those things.

Sam King's job was to make new highways, or make old highways wider. His bulldozer ripped into the earth and pushed big mounds of dirt and rock to one side.

When he was finished, the steamrollers came and made the highway smooth and flat. When cars went past, Sam sometimes waved to the children inside. But mostly he kept his eyes on his work, pulling and pushing the levers that operated the giant bulldozer.

Sam liked his big bulldozer. Once a week he climbed all over it, greasing and oiling it. Sam looked after that machine as if it were his own. He liked making new highways, too. But what he didn't like were the steamrollers and trucks working all around him. The dust and noise were terrible. He wore earmuffs to keep out the noise. And when the dust was especially thick, he wore a mask over his mouth.

Another thing Sam didn't like about his job was that the new highways, or changes to the old highways, were a long way from town.

He had to leave his house early in the morning, and he didn't get back until late at night. That didn't give him much time for making things in his workshop.

Chapter Two
A Bulldozer of His Own

One night Sam put down the newspaper he was reading.

"I think I'll give up working on the highways," he said to Mrs. King.

Mrs. King was reading a book. She looked across at Sam.

"Stop working?!" she asked.

"No, just find another job," said Sam.

"But what else can you do?" said Mrs. King, raising her voice a little. "You've been driving a bulldozer for years."

"And I still want to drive one," said Sam. "But I'd like a bulldozer of my own. And I want to work around town."

Mrs. King seemed puzzled. "What could that big machine do in town?" she asked.

Sam smiled. "Wait and see," he said.

So Sam gave up his job on the roads. The boss and the other highway workers were sorry to see him go.

"It won't seem the same without you, Sam," they said. "You've worked on the highway crew longer than anyone else."

Then Sam went looking for a bulldozer of his own. The man who sold bulldozers in town showed him everything he had. The big machines were lined up in the parking lot like a row of monsters waiting to bite great chunks out of the earth. And each one cost thousands of dollars, far more money than Sam could afford to pay.

"These are too big," said Sam. "I want a small bulldozer, one that I can put on a trailer behind my truck."

The man shook his head. "Well now, I don't know about that," he said. "Everyone wants bigger and bigger machines these days."

"I don't," said Sam. "The smaller, the better for me.
And I don't want a noisy machine."

The bulldozer salesman shook his head again.
"Sorry, Sam," he said.

Just as Sam was getting in his truck, the salesman called out.

"Hold on. A long time ago, we *did* have a little old machine, but it broke down and no one could fix it. I think it's in our scrap heap."

So Sam King and the salesman went around to the back of the shop to have a look at the scrap heap.

Chapter Three

Just a Piece of Junk?

The scrap heap was a pile of old bulldozer parts. There were rusted blades, parts of tracks, iron bars, dented cabs, and worn bolts.

"I'm sure it's still here," said the salesman, peering into the pile of rubbish.

Sam lifted a twisted sheet of iron, and there it was–a bulldozer. A small bulldozer. A *very* small bulldozer. A very old, very battered small bulldozer, red with rust.

Sam shoved aside some more pieces of junk so that he could get a better look at the little machine. Soon he had uncovered it.

"There are a few parts missing," said the salesman. "That's why it's in the scrap heap."

Sam looked long and hard at the little bulldozer. Could he get the engine running? Could he make parts for the pieces that were missing? He stood there, wondering.

Finally, Sam pushed back his hat and scratched his head.

"How much?" he asked.

The salesman laughed. "That little thing is just a piece of junk," he said. "You can have it. We'll be glad to get rid of it."

"I'll give it a try," said Sam. "But it's going to be a big job."

"A hopeless job, if you ask me," said the salesman. "Would you like some help putting it on your trailer?"

"Yes, please," said Sam.

The salesman called to another man with a front-end loader, and in no time at all the little bulldozer was lifted up onto Sam's trailer.

Chapter Four

Little Bull Comes to Life!

Sam drove home slowly. Although the little bulldozer wasn't big, it was very heavy.

"Heavens!" cried Mrs. King when she saw it. "I hope you didn't buy that old thing!"

"Of course not," said Sam, grinning. "I got it for nothing."

"I should think so," said Mrs. King. And she went back into the house, shaking her head.

Unloading the little bulldozer in the workshop was quite a big job. Sam tipped up his trailer and let the machine slide down. Then he pulled the trailer forward with his truck. But the back of the trailer broke, and the bulldozer landed on the workshop floor with a great THUD!

Then Sam started the important job of rebuilding the bulldozer.

First, he took the engine apart, piece by piece. After he had cleaned and oiled each piece, he put the engine back together again and started it up.

Suddenly, the little engine came to life–not with a
roar, but with a low growl that sounded wonderful
to Sam.

Then he scraped the rust from the parts of the machine that were scattered on the workshop floor. He figured out which parts were missing. It was like a giant puzzle. And even though Sam knew all about bulldozers, he scratched his head several times before he had it figured out.

When he knew what he needed, he went all over town looking for parts. Each day he came home with a different bit or piece. None of them belonged on the little bulldozer, but Sam knew how to change them to make them fit.

Chapter Five

Sam King and Little Bull:
One Great Team!

At last, the little machine began to look like a real bulldozer. Sam walked around it and smiled. This was just what he wanted. The little bulldozer looked a little strange, but he knew it would do the jobs he wanted it to do.

It took Sam a few more days to paint the little bulldozer a bright yellow color. And the more he worked on the machine, the more he liked it.

There was a blade on the front of the machine, but Sam exchanged that for a set of steel jaws that looked like giant teeth. It didn't take long. And now Sam had the machine he had always wanted.

"There aren't many machines like this around,"
Sam told Mrs. King.

"I agree," she said, shaking her head.

"But it looks so small," said Mrs. King. "Are you
sure it will do anything?"

"It will do everything I want it to," said Sam.

"Soon, I hope," said Mrs. King. "We're running
out of money!"

Then, with the little bulldozer on his trailer, Sam went out looking for jobs to do.

"Sorry," said the city engineer. "We've got our own bulldozer."

"Sorry," said the head of the workers clearing land for a new building near the post office. "We need a big machine for this job."

As Sam drove away, he heard the men laughing and pointing at his little bulldozer.

Poor Sam. Nobody, it seemed, had any work for such a little machine.

As he started to drive home, he felt very sad.

But on the way home, Sam saw a man digging at a hillside behind a house. Sam parked in front of the house and walked around to talk with the man.

"It will take a long time for you to dig out that hillside," said Sam.

The man approached him, rubbing his aching back.
"You're telling me," he said. "I really need a bulldozer,
but there isn't enough room to get one around the
side of the house."

"I have a machine that can get in here," said Sam.

After that, Sam found plenty of work in places where big machines couldn't go.

He was happy. He kept his little bulldozer clean and oiled. One night he painted a name on its yellow cab: Little Bull!

"You may not be big and strong, but you can go anywhere," Sam said, rubbing a cloth over the machine's clean surface.

"And you know something? We're going to make a great team, you and I."